CORAL SNAKES

THE SNAKE DISCOVERY LIBRARY

Sherie Bargar   Linda Johnson

Photographer/Consultant: George Van Horn

Watermill Press
Mahwah, New Jersey

© 1987 Rourke Enterprises, Inc.

All rights reserved. No part of this book may be reproduced or utilized in any form or by any means, electronic or mechanical including photocopying, recording or by any information storage and retrieval system without permission in writing from the publisher.

Library of Congress Cataloging in Publication Data

Bargar, Sherie, 1944-
  Coral snakes.

  (The Snake discovery library)
  Includes index.
  Summary: An introduction to the physical characteristics, habits, natural environment, and relationship to human beings of the various species of coral snakes.
  1. Micrurus—Juvenile literature. 2. Snakes—Juvenile literature. [1. Coral snakes. 2. Snakes] I. Johnson, Linda, 1947-   . II. Van Horn, George, ill. III. Title. IV. Series: Bargar, Sherie, 1944-   . Snake discovery library.
QL666.064B3725   1987   597.96   87-12710
ISBN 0-86592-246-2

Title Photo:
Central American Bicolor Coral Snake
Micrurus mipartitus

TABLE OF CONTENTS

Coral Snakes	5
Where They Live	6
How They Look	9
Their Senses	11
The Head and Mouth	14
Baby Coral Snakes	16
Prey	19
Their Defenses	20
Coral Snakes and People	22
Glossary	23
Index	24

CORAL SNAKES

Although there are up to 50 species of **poisonous** coral snakes, only the Arizona and Eastern Coral Snake are found in the United States. Coral snakes are the only members of the *Elapidae* family that are found in North, Central, and South America. They do not inhabit any other region of the world. Vivid red, yellow, and black bands characterize the colorful Eastern Coral Snake. Many nonpoisonous snakes like the Scarlet Kingsnake have similar color patterns. The easiest way to identify the coral snake is to check the order of its colored bands. Like a traffic light, the Eastern Coral Snake has its red and yellow colors side by side.

Central American Coral Snake
Micrurus nigrocinctus

WHERE THEY LIVE

The Arizona Coral Snake prefers a dry, arid **habitat** and is seldom seen by people. The larger and more familiar Eastern Coral Snake often lies beneath decayed vegetation near water. The Eastern Coral Snake geographically ranges from the southern part of North Carolina to the southern tip of Florida. It lives as far west as Texas. The South American corals often **burrow** and can be found beneath the bark of trees. A few South American species prefer an aquatic environment and feed on fish. Coral snakes often hide in their **habitat** which makes it possible for them to live very near people without being seen.

Eastern Coral Snake
Micrurus fuluius

HOW THEY LOOK

All species of coral snakes have slender bodies with blunt heads and tiny eyes. Adults of the species average 2 feet in length. Some of the South American species have reached lengths of over 5 feet. The longest known Eastern Coral Snake measured 47½ inches. The smooth glossy scales of the coral snakes' bodies are patterned with bands of 2 or 3 colors. All species begin their patterns with a black nose. The head and tail of the Eastern Coral Snake have black and yellow bands. The body adds red bands and begins a pattern of red-yellow-black-yellow.

Eastern Coral Snake
Micrurus fuluius

THEIR SENSES

The coral snake relies on its sense of smell more than any other sense to find **prey**. The coral snake's tongue flicks out and brings in particles from surrounding areas. The Jacobson's organ in the roof of the mouth **analyzes** the particles to learn what is nearby. The coral snake is unable to focus well, but it can detect movement at close range. The ground **vibration** of oncoming animals is felt by the snake and helps it to flee from enemies.

Eastern Coral Snake
Micrurus fuluius

Scarlet Kingsnake
Lampropeltis triangulum elapsoides

Eastern Coral Snake
Micrurus fuluius

THE HEAD AND MOUTH

The coral snake's small head has a blunt nose. Short, hollow fangs are fixed to the front of the upper jaw. **Venom** glands on each side of the head are located behind the eyes. Muscles around the **venom** glands pump **venom** through a **duct** to the fangs. The **venom paralyzes** the **prey**. The **paralysis** is caused by an element of the **venom** which blocks signals from the nerves to the muscles. The coral snake stretches its jaws like a rubber band and swallows the paralyzed victim whole. While swallowing the **prey**, the windpipe extends from the throat to the front of the mouth and allows the snake to breathe.

Eastern Coral Snake
Micrurus fuluius

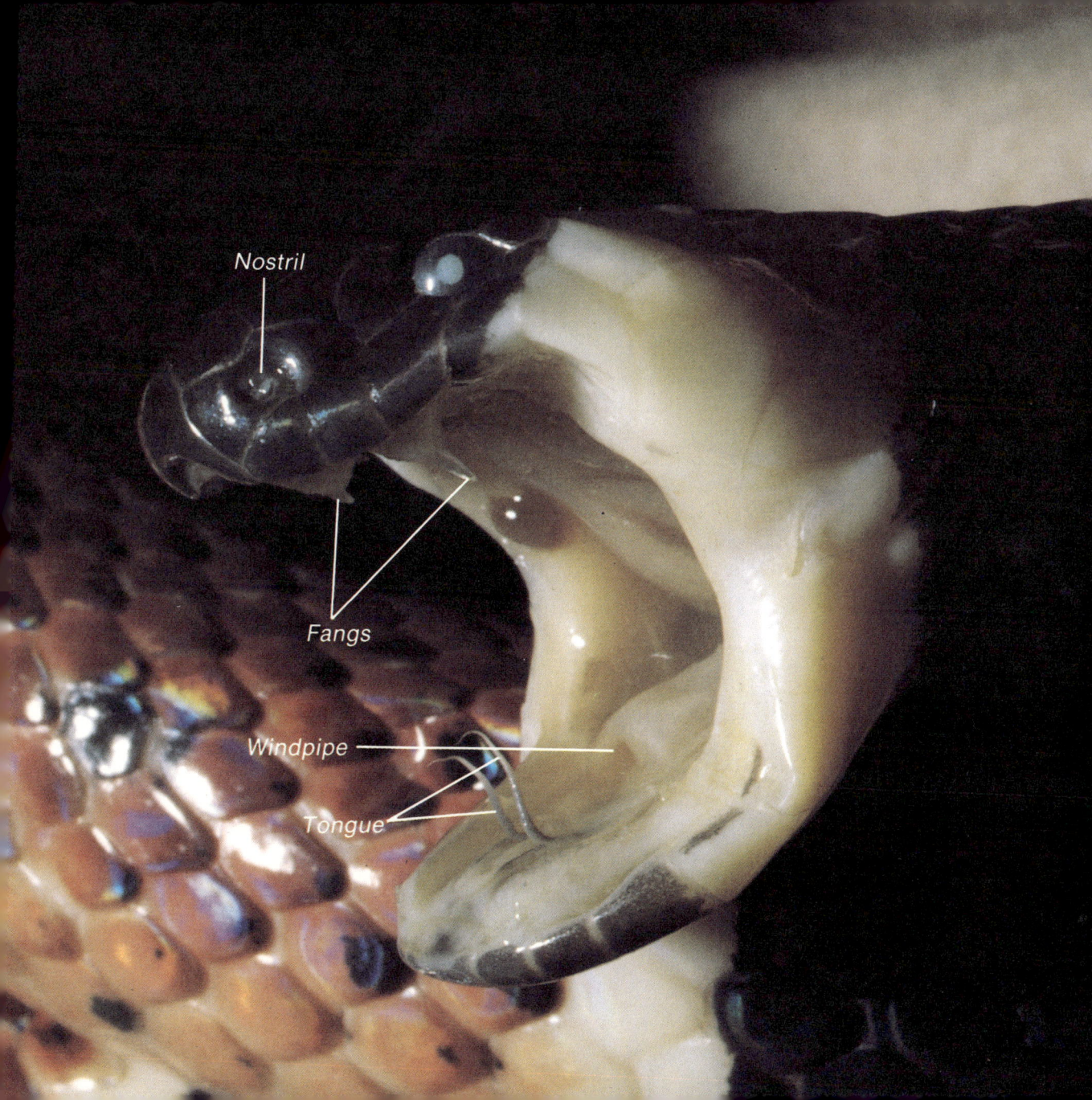

BABY CORAL SNAKES

Coral snakes are seen most often during the spring. It is during this season that coral snakes mate. In the summer, mother coral snakes search for decaying vegetation which will provide warmth and humidity suitable for her eggs to develop. The mother coral snake will lay 6 to 12 eggs. They hatch into small, brightly colored baby coral snakes in about 2 months. The babies are about 6 inches long and weigh less than half an ounce. From birth they are capable of killing **prey** and defending themselves.

Eastern Coral Snake
Micrurus fuluius

Central American Tricolor Coral Snake
Micrurus nigrocinctus

PREY

Lizards and other snakes are the **prey** of coral snakes. Most coral snakes will even eat their look-alike, the Scarlet Kingsnake. Coral snakes are daytime hunters taking advantage of any passing **prey**. Birds and many small animals eat the coral snake. However, it is possible for the coral snake to bite and kill the enemy even as it is being swallowed. It is believed that many potential **predators** recognize the bright colors of the coral snake as a sign of danger and avoid it.

Eastern Coral Snake
Micrurus fuluius

THEIR DEFENSE

In spite of the brilliant colors, it is often difficult to see the coral snake as it moves rapidly across the forest floor. Lying beneath vegetation, the coral snake is not easily seen by its enemies. Hiding is its best defense. When confronted by an enemy, the clever coral snake often hides its head. It forms a circle with its tail causing the enemy to focus its attention on the tail. This behavior confuses the enemy and gives the snake time to find an escape.

Eastern Coral Snake
Micrurus fuluius

CORAL SNAKES AND PEOPLE

People in the southeastern part of the United States fear the Eastern Coral Snake because of its notoriously **toxic venom**. Because of its small size, it usually does not **inject** enough **venom** to cause death in a human. When bitten, there is usually plenty of time to seek medical assistance. Usually the shy coral snake avoids humans and is reluctant to bite. Mistaking a coral snake for one of its look-alikes, people are often bitten when they attempt to handle it as they would a **nonvenomous** snake.

GLOSSARY

analyze (AN a lyze) analyzes — To find out what something is.

burrow (BUR row) — A hole dug in the ground by an animal.

duct (DUCT) — A tube through which liquids pass.

habitat (HAB i tat) — A place where an animal lives.

inject (in JECT) — Pump in.

nonvenomous (non VEN om ous) — Does not cause sickness or death.

paralysis (pa RAL y sis) paralyzes — Lack of feeling or movement.

poison (POI son) poisonous — A substance that causes sickness or death when it enters the body.

predator (PRED a tor) predators — An animal that eats other animals.

prey (PREY) — An animal hunted or killed by another animal for food.

toxic (TOX ic) — Harmful.

venom (VEN om) — A chemical made in animals that makes other animals and people sick or kills them.

vibrate (VI brate) vibration — To move back and forth.

INDEX

Arizona Coral Snake 5, 6
Babies 16
Body 5, 14
Color 5, 9, 14
Defense 20
Eastern Coral Snake 5, 6, 9
Fangs 14
Habitat 6
Head 9, 14
Jacobson's organ 11
Length 9
Mouth 14
Prey 6, 19
Scarlet Kingsnake 5, 19
Sight 11
Smell 11
Tongue 11
Venom 14, 22